MOTHER GOOSE

NURSERY RHYMES

MOTHER GOOSE
NURSERY RHYMES

ILLUSTRATED BY
ARTHUR RACKHAM

A STUDIO BOOK
THE VIKING PRESS · NEW YORK

Published in 1975 by The Viking Press, Inc.
625 Madison Avenue, New York, N.Y. 10022
Printed in U.S.A.

Library of Congress Cataloging in Publication Data
Mother Goose.
    Mother Goose nursery rhymes.

  (A Studio book)
    Includes index.
    Summary: A collection of 162 nursery rhymes illustrated
by Arthur Rackham.

    1. Nursery rhymes. [1. Nursery rhymes]   I. Rack-
ham, Arthur, 1867-1939. II. Title.
PZ8.3.M85Rac6   398.8   75-16242
ISBN 0-670-49003-2

LIST OF ILLUSTRATIONS
IN COLOR

ABOUT THIS BOOK

THERE are many more Nursery Rhymes than are included in this book, though I think most of the best known are here. I have chosen those I knew and liked best in my own nursery days, and I have kept to the versions that I was familiar with. I think one may do so, as nursery rhymes have until recently been handed on only by oral tradition with its inevitable variations. At home we had no complete book of them: most we knew came direct from our elders. The children of the present day often have several different printed versions of the same rhyme, but they do not seem to be confused by them. They make their own choice, and go on inventing variations. And however much they alter and add to our old friend Mother Goose's original collection, they still make use of her name.

S EE, saw, Margery Daw,
Johnny shall have a new master;
He shall have but a penny a day,
Because he can't work any faster.

I'LL tell you a story
About Jack-a-Nory,—
And now my story's begun:
I'll tell you another
About Jack and his brother,—
And now my story's done.

JACK SPRAT could eat no fat,
His wife could eat no lean:
And so, betwixt them both,
They lick'd the platter clean.

SEE, saw, Margery Daw
Sold her bed and lay upon straw.
Was not she a dirty slut,
To sell her bed and lie in the dirt!

PAT-A-CAKE, pat-a-cake, baker's man!
Make me a cake as fast as you can:
Prick it and stick it, and mark it with B,
And put it in the oven for Baby and me.

ROCK-A-BYE, baby, thy cradle is green;
Father's a nobleman, mother's a queen;
And Betty's a lady, and wears a gold ring;
And Johnny's a drummer, and drums for the king.

Little Bo-peep

ITTLE BO-PEEP has lost her sheep,
And can't tell where to find them;
Leave them alone, and they'll come home,
And bring their tails behind them.

Little Bo-Peep fell fast asleep,
And dreamt she heard them bleating;
But when she awoke she found it a joke,
For they were still a-fleeting.

Then up she took her little crook,
Determined for to find them;
She found them indeed, but it made her heart bleed,
For they'd left their tails behind them.

R IDE a cock-horse to Banbury Cross,
To see a fine lady upon a white horse;
With rings on her fingers and bells on her toes,
She shall have music wherever she goes.

Bye, baby bunting.
Daddy's gone a hunting,
To get a little rabbit's skin
To wrap the baby bunting in.

A GAME WITH THE FACE

Ring the bell!   *Giving a lock of the hair a pull*
Knock at the door!   *Tapping the forehead*
Draw the latch!   *Pulling up the nose*
And walk in!   *Opening the mouth and putting*
in the finger

How many days has my baby to play?
Saturday, Sunday, Monday,
Tuesday, Wednesday, Thursday, Friday,
Saturday, Sunday, Monday.

Mary had a little lamb,
With fleece as white as snow;
And everywhere that Mary went,
The lamb was sure to go.

It followed her to school one day,
Which was against the rule.
And made the children laugh and play,
To see a lamb at school.

And so the teacher turned it out,
But still it lingered near,
And waited patiently about,
Till Mary did appear.

"What makes the lamb love Mary so?"
The eager children cry,
"Why, Mary loves the lamb, you know!"
The teacher did reply.

Sing a song of sixpence,
A pocket full of rye;
Four and twenty blackbirds
Baked in a pie;

When the pie was open'd,
The birds began to sing;
Was not that a dainty dish,
To set before the king?

The king was in his counting-house
Counting out his money;
The queen was in the parlour
Eating bread and honey;

The maid was in the garden
Hanging out the clothes,
There came a little blackbird,
And snapped off her nose.

Hush-a-bye, baby, on the tree top;
When the wind blows, the cradle will rock;
When the bough breaks, the cradle will fall;
Down will come baby, and cradle, and all.

GOOSEY, goosey, gander,
Whither shall I wander?
Upstairs and downstairs,
And in my lady's chamber.
There I met an old man
That wouldn't say his prayers;
I took him by the left leg,
And threw him downstairs.

DANTY, baby, diddy,
What shall its mammy do wid'e?
Sit in a lap,
And give it some pap,
Danty, baby, diddy.

LITTLE Betty Blue
Lost her holiday shoe,
What will poor Betty do?
Why, give her another,
To match the other,
And then she may walk in two.

ONE misty, moisty morning,
When cloudy was the weather,
There I met an old man
Clothed all in leather;

Clothed all in leather,
With cap under his chin,—
How do you do, and how do you do,
And how do you do again!

THREE little kittens they lost their mittens,
And they began to cry,
Oh! mother dear,
We very much fear,
That we have lost our mittens.
What! lost your mittens, you naughty kittens,
Then you shall have no pie.
Mee-ow, mee-ow, mee-ow.
Yes, you shall have no pie.
Mee-ow, mee-ow, mee-ow.

Three little kittens they found their mittens,
And they began to cry,
Oh! mother dear,
See here, see here,
See, we have found our mittens,
What! found your mittens, you little kittens,
Then you shall have some pie.
Purr, purr, purr.
Yes, you shall have some pie.
Purr, purr, purr.

The three little kittens put on their mittens,
And soon ate up the pie;
Oh! mother dear,
We greatly fear,
That we have soiled our mittens.
What! soiled your mittens! you naughty kittens!
Then they began to sigh,
Miow, miow, miow,
Then they began to sigh,
Miow, miow, miow.

The three little kittens, they washed their mittens,
And hung them out to dry;
Oh! mother dear,
Look here, look here,
See, we have washed our mittens.
What! washed your mittens, you darling kittens,
But I smell a rat close by,
Hush! hush! miew, miew,
We smell a rat close by,
Miew, miew, miew.

To market, to market,
To buy a plum cake;
Home again, home again,
Market's late.

To market, to market,
To buy a plum bun;
Home again, home again,
Market's done.

JACK and Jill went up the hill
To fetch a pail of water;
Jack fell down and broke his crown,
And Jill came tumbling after.

Then up Jack got and home did trot
As fast as he could caper;
And went to bed to mend his head
With vinegar and brown paper.

RUB a dub dub,
Three men in a tub:
And who do you think they be
The butcher, the baker,
The candlestick-maker;
Turn 'em out, knaves all three.

Monday's bairn is fair of face,
Tuesday's bairn is full of grace,
Wednesday's bairn is full of woe,
Thursday's bairn has far to go,
Friday's bairn is loving and giving,
Saturday's bairn works hard for its living.
But the bairn that is born on the Sabbath day
Is bonny and blithe, and good and gay.

Come when you're called,
Do as you're bid,
Shut the door after you,
Never be chid.

EE-SAW sacradown,
Which is the way to London town?
One foot up and the other foot down,
That is the way to London town.

GEORGIE PORGIE, pudding and pie,
Kissed the girls and made them cry;
When the girls begin to play,
Georgie Porgie runs away.

To market, to market, to buy a fat pig;
Home again, home again, dancing a jig,
To market, to market, to buy a fat hog;
Home again, home again, jiggety-jog.

J‍ACK, be nimble,
And, Jack, be quick;
And, Jack, jump over
The candlestick.

DOCTOR FOSTER went to Glo'ster
In a shower of rain;
He stepped in a puddle, right up to his middle,
And never went there again.

SING, sing, what shall I sing?
The cat's run off with the pudding-bag string!
Do, do, what shall I do?
The cat has bitten it quite in two.

ICKETY, Pickety,
My black hen,
She lays eggs
For gentlemen;
Sometimes ninè,
And sometimes ten.
Hickety, Pickety,
My black hen!

I LOVE little pussy, her coat is so warm:
And if I don't hurt her she'll do me no harm.
So I won't pull her tail nor drive her away,
But pussy and I very gently will play.

HICKORY, Dickory, Dock,
The mouse ran up the clock;
The clock struck one;
The mouse ran down;
Hickory, Dickory, Dock.

DANCE to your daddy,
My little babby;
Dance to your daddy,
My little lamb.
You shall have a fishy
In a little dishy;
You shall have a fishy
When the boat comes in.

ARBER, barber, shave a pig;
How many hairs will make a wig?
Four-and-twenty, that's enough:
Give the barber a pinch of snuff.

PEASE-PUDDING hot,
Pease-pudding cold,
Pease-pudding in the pot,
Nine days old.
Some like it hot,
Some like it cold,
Some like it in the pot,
Nine days old.

ONE to make ready,
And two to prepare;
Good luck to the rider,
And away goes the mare.

HERE we go round the mulberry bush,
The mulberry bush, the mulberry bush,
Here we go round the mulberry bush,
On a cold and frosty morning.

Jack Sprat and his wife

Bye, baby bunting

Jack and Jill

Little Miss Muffett

This is the way we wash our hands,
Wash our hands, wash our hands,
This is the way we wash our hands,
On a cold and frosty morning.

This is the way we wash our clothes,
Wash our clothes, wash our clothes,
This is the way we wash our clothes,
On a cold and frosty morning.

This is the way we go to school,
Go to school, go to school,
This is the way we go to school,
On a cold and frosty morning.

This is the way we come out of school,
Come out of school, come out of school,
This is the way we come out of school,
On a cold and frosty morning.

*And anything else children can act while they sing. The first
verse sung again after each of the others, while the children dance.*

A WAS an Archer, and shot at a frog,

B was a Butcher, and had a great dog.

C was a Captain, all covered with lace,

D was a Drummer, and had a red face.

E was an Esquire, with pride on his brow,

F was a Farmer, and followed the plough.

G was a Gamester, who had but ill luck,

H was a Hunter, and hunted a buck.

I was an Innkeeper, who loved to bouse,

J was a Joiner, and built up a house.

K was a King, so mighty and grand,

L was a Lady who had a white hand.

M was a Miser, and hoarded up gold,

N was a Nobleman, gallant and bold.

O was an Oyster Wench, and went about town,

P was a Parson, and wore a black gown.

Q was a Queen, who was fond of good flip,

R was a Robber, and wanted a whip.

S was a Sailor, who spent all he got,

T was a Tinker, and mended a pot.

U was an Usurer, a miserable elf,

V was a Vintner, who drank all himself.

W was a Watchman, and guarded the door,

X was expensive, and so became poor.

Y was a Youth, that did not love school,

Z was a Zany, a poor harmless fool.

LITTLE Miss Muffett
Sat on a tuffet,
Eating her curds and whey;
There came a great spider,
And sat down beside her,
And frightened Miss Muffett away.

THE girl in the lane, that couldn't speak plain
Cried, "Gobble, gobble, gobble."
The man on the hill, that couldn't stand still,
Went hobble, hobble, hobble.

ONE, two,
Buckle my shoe;
Three, four,
Knock at the door;
Five, six,
Pick up sticks;
Seven, eight,
Lay them straight;
Nine, ten,
A good fat hen.
Eleven, twelve,
Dig and delve;
Thirteen, fourteen,
Maids a-courting;
Fifteen, sixteen,
Maids in the kitchen;
Seventeen, eighteen,
Maids a-waiting;
Nineteen, twenty,
My plate's empty.

THERE was a little boy and a little girl
Lived in an alley;
Says the little boy to the girl,
"Shall I, oh! shall I?"
Says the little girl to the little boy,
"What shall we do?"
Says the little boy to the little girl,
"I will kiss you."

DIDDLETY, diddlety, dumpty;
The cat ran up the plum-tree.
Half-a-crown
To fetch her down;
Diddlety, diddlety, dumpty.

ONE, two, three, four, five,
Catching fishes all alive!
"Why did you let them go?"
"Because they bit my finger so."
"Which finger did they bite?"
"The little finger on the right."

LONG legs, crooked thighs,
Little head, and no eyes.
                              [*Pair of tongs*.

MARY, Mary, quite contrary,
How does your garden grow?
With cockle-shells, and silver bells,
And pretty maids all in a row.

R AIN, rain, go to Spain,
Don't come back again!

S OLOMON GRUNDY,
Born on a Monday,
Christened on Tuesday,
Married on Wednesday,
Took ill on Thursday,
Worse on Friday,
Died on Saturday,
Buried on Sunday:
This is the end
Of Solomon Grundy.

Ding, dong, bell,
Pussy's in the well!
Who put her in?—
Little Tommy Green.
Who pulled her out?—
Little Johnny Stout.
What a naughty boy was that
To try to drown poor pussy-cat,
Who never did any harm,
But kill'd the mice in his father's barn.

This is the house that Jack built.

2. This is the malt
   That lay in the house that Jack built.

3. This is the rat,
   That ate the malt,
   That lay in the house that Jack built.

4. This is the cat,
   That kill'd the rat,
   That ate the malt,
   That lay in the house that Jack built.

5. This is the dog,
   That worried the cat,
   That kill'd the rat,
   That ate the malt,
   That lay in the house that Jack built.

6. This is the cow with the crumpled horn,
   That toss'd the dog,
   That worried the cat,
   That kill'd the rat,
   That ate the malt,
   That lay in the house that Jack built.

7. This is the maiden, all forlorn,
   That milk'd the cow with the crumpled horn,
   That tossed the dog,
   That worried the cat,
   That kill'd the rat,
   That ate the malt,
   That lay in the house that Jack built.

8. This is the man all tatter'd and torn,
   That kissed the maiden all forlorn,
   That milk'd the cow with the crumpled horn,
   That tossed the dog,
   That worried the cat,
   That kill'd the rat,
   That ate the malt,
   That lay in the house that Jack built.

9. This is the priest all shaven and shorn,
   That married the man all tatter'd and torn,
   That kiss'd the maiden all forlorn,
   That milk'd the cow with the crumpled horn,
   That tossed the dog,
   That worried the cat,
   That kill'd the rat,
   That ate the malt,
   That lay in the house that Jack built.

10. This is the cock that crow'd in the morn,
    That waked the priest all shaven and shorn,
    That married the man all tatter'd and torn,
    That kiss'd the maiden all forlorn,
    That milk'd the cow with the crumpled horn,
    That tossed the dog,
    That worried the cat,
    That kill'd the rat,
    That ate the malt,
    That lay in the house that Jack built.

11. This is the farmer sowing his corn,
    That kept the cock that crow'd in the morn,
    That waked the priest all shaven and shorn,
    That married the man all tatter'd and torn,
    That kiss'd the maiden all forlorn,
    That milk'd the cow with the crumpled horn,
    That tossed the dog,
    That worried the cat,
    That kill'd the rat,
    That ate the malt,
    That lay in the house that Jack built.

PETER PIPER picked a peck of pickled pepper;
A peck of pickled pepper Peter Piper picked;
If Peter Piper picked a peck of pickled pepper;
Where's the peck of pickled pepper Peter Piper picked?

THERE was an old woman who lived in a shoe;
She had so many children she didn't know what to do;
She gave them some broth without any bread,
And whipped them all soundly and put them to bed.

Hᴇʏ! diddle, diddle,
The cat and the fiddle,
The cow jumped over the moon;
The little dog laugh'd
To see such sport,
And the dish ran away with the spoon.

Dᴀɴᴄᴇ, Thumbkin, dance;
              [Keep the thumb in motion.

Dance, ye merrymen, every one;
              [All the fingers in motion.

For Thumbkin, he can dance alone,
              [The thumb only moving.

Thumbkin, he can dance alone,   *[Ditto.*
Dance, Foreman, dance,   *[The first finger moving.*
Dance, ye merrymen, every one;
              [The whole moving.

But, Foreman, he can dance alone;
Foreman, he can dance alone.

[And so on with the others, naming the second finger "Longman," the third finger "Ringman," and the fourth finger "Littleman." "Ringman" cannot dance alone.]

A APPLE-PIE;
B bit it;
C cut it;
D dealt it;
E ate it;
F fought for it;
G got it;
H had it;
J joined it;
K kept it;
L longed for it;
M mourned for it;
N nodded at it;
O opened it;
P peeped in it;
Q quartered it;
R ran for it;
S stole for it;
T took it;
V viewed it;
W wanted it;
X, Y, Z, and amperse-and,
All wished for a piece in hand.

Johnny shall have a new bonnet
And Johnny shall go to the fair,
And Johnny shall have a blue ribbon
To tie up his bonny brown hair.

And why may not I love Johnny?
And why may not Johnny love me?
And why may not I love Johnny
As well as another body?

And here's a leg for a stocking,
And here's a leg for a shoe,
And he has a kiss for his daddy,
And two for his mammy, I trow.

And why may not I love Johnny?
And why may not Johnny love me?
And why may not I love Johnny,
As well as another body?

THREE blind mice,
Three blind mice,
See how they run!
See how they run!
They all ran after the farmer's wife,
Who cut off their tails with a carving-knife;
Did you ever see such fun in your life
As three blind mice?

A LITTLE cock-sparrow sat on a green tree,
And he chirruped, he chirruped, so merry was he;
A naughty boy came with his wee bow and arrow,
Determined to shoot this little cock-sparrow;

"This little cock-sparrow shall make me a stew,
And his giblets shall make me a little pie too";
"Oh, no," said the sparrow, "I *won't* make a stew";
So he flapped his wings, and away he flew.

GREAT A, little a,
Bouncing B!
The cat's in the cupboard,
And can't see me.

ELISABETH, Elspeth, Betsy, and
Bess,
They all went together to seek a bird's
nest.
They found a bird's nest with five eggs in,
They all took one, and left four in.

I saw three ships come sailing by,
Come sailing by, come sailing by;
I saw three ships come sailing by,
On New Year's Day in the morning.

And what do you think was in them then,
Was in them then, was in them then?
And what do you think was in them then,
On New Year's Day in the morning?

Three pretty girls were in them then,
Were in them then, were in them then;
Three pretty girls were in them then,
On New Year's Day in the morning.

And one could whistle, and one could sing,
And one could play on the violin—
Such joy there was at my wedding,
On New Year's Day in the morning.

LITTLE Tom Tucker
Sang for his supper;
What shall he eat?
White bread and butter.
How shall he cut it,
Without e'er a knife?
How shall he marry
Without e'er a wife?

THIS is the way the ladies ride:
Tri, tre, tre, tree,
Tri, tre, tre, tree!
This is the way the ladies ride:
Tri, tre, tre, tre, tri-tre-tre-tree!

This is the way the gentlemen ride:
Gallop-a-trot,
Gallop-a-trot!
This is the way the gentlemen ride:
Gallop-a-gallop-a-trot!

This is the way the farmers ride:
Hobbledy-hoy,
Hobbledy-hoy!
This is the way the farmers ride:
Hobbledy hobbledy-hoy!

CROSS Patch,
Lift the latch,
Sit by the fire and spin;
Take a cup,
And drink it up,
Then call your neighbours in.

WHEN good King Arthur ruled this land,
He was a goodly king;
He stole three pecks of barley-meal,
To make a bag-pudding.

A bag-pudding the king did make,
And stuff'd it well with plums.
And in it put great lumps of fat,
As big as my two thumbs.

The king and queen did eat thereof,
And noblemen beside;
And what they could not eat that night,
The queen next morning fried.

POLLY put the kettle on,
Polly put the kettle on,
Polly put the kettle on,
We'll all have tea.

Sukey take it off again,
Sukey take it off again,
Sukey take it off again,
They're all gone away.

Hark, hark, the dogs do bark,
The beggars are coming to town.
Some in rags, and some in tags,
And some in velvet gown.

"Where are you going to, my pretty maid?"
"I'm going a-milking, sir," she said.

"May I go with you, my pretty maid?"
"You're kindly welcome, sir," she said.

"What is your father, my pretty maid?"
"My father's a farmer, sir," she said.

"What is your fortune, my pretty maid?"
"My face is my fortune, sir," she said.

"Then I can't marry you, my pretty maid!"
"Nobody asked you, sir," she said.

Baa, baa, black sheep,
Have you any wool?
"Yes, sir, yes, sir,
Three bags full:
One for my master,
And one for my dame,
And one for the little boy
Who lives in the lane."

LITTLE Tommy Tittlemouse
Lived in a little house;
He caught fishes
In other men's ditches.

CRY, baby, cry,
Put your finger in your eye.
And tell your mother it wasn't I.

Rain, rain, go to Spain

Hey! diddle, diddle!

Hark ! hark ! the dogs do bark

*There was an old woman
Lived under a hill*

IF I'd as much money as I could spend,
I never would cry old chairs to mend;
Old chairs to mend, old chairs to mend,
I never would cry, old chairs to mend.

If I'd as much money as I could tell,
I never would cry young lambs to sell;
Young lambs to sell, young lambs to sell,
I never would cry young lambs to sell.

THE Queen of Hearts,
She made some tarts,
All on a summer's day;
The Knave of Hearts,
He stole those tarts,
And took them clean away.

The King of Hearts
Called for the tarts,
And beat the Knave full sore;
The Knave of Hearts
Brought back the tarts,
And vowed he'd steal no more.

A DILLAR, a dollar,
A ten o'clock scholar,
What makes you come so soon?
You used to come at ten o'clock,
But now you come at noon.

THE lion and the unicorn
Were fighting for the crown;
The lion beat the unicorn
All round the town.

Some gave them white bread,
And some gave them brown;
Some gave them plum-cake,
And drummed them out of town.

THERE was a little man,
And he had a little gun,
And his bullets were made of lead, lead, lead;
He went to the brook
And he saw a little duck,
And he shot it right through the head, head, head.

He carried it home
To his old wife Joan,
And he bid her a fire for to make, make, make;
To roast the little duck
He had shot in the brook,
And he'd go and fetch her the drake, drake, drake.

I LOVE sixpence, pretty little sixpence,
I love sixpence better than my life;
I spent a penny of it, I spent another,
And I took fourpence home to my wife.

Oh, my little fourpence, pretty little fourpence,
I love fourpence better than my life;
I spent a penny of it, I spent another,
And I took twopence home to my wife.

Oh, my little twopence, my pretty little twopence,
I love twopence better than my life;
I spent a penny of it, I spent another,
And I took nothing home to my wife.

Oh, my little nothing, my pretty little nothing,
What will nothing buy for my wife?
I have nothing, I spend nothing,
I love nothing better than my wife.

THERE was an old woman, as I've heard tell,
She went to market her eggs for to sell;
She went to market all on a market-day,
And she fell asleep on the king's highway.

There came by a pedlar whose name was Stout;
He cut her petticoats all round about;
He cut her petticoats up to the knees,
Which made the old woman to shiver and freeze.

When this little woman first did wake,
She began to shiver and she began to shake;
She began to wonder and she began to cry,
"Oh! deary, deary me, this is none of I!

"But if it be I, as I do hope it be,
I've a little dog at home, and he'll know me;
If it be I, he'll wag his little tail,
And if it be not I, he'll loudly bark and wail."

Home went the little woman all in the dark;
Up got the little dog and he began to bark;
He began to bark, so she began to cry,
"Oh! deary, deary me, this is none of I!"

Tom, Tom, the piper's son,
Stole a pig, and away he run!
The pig was eat, and Tom was beat,
And Tom went roaring down the street.

Tom he was a piper's son,
He learn'd to play when he was young,
But all the tunes that he could play,
Was "Over the hills and far away";
Over the hills and a great way off,
And the wind will blow my top-knot off.

Now Tom with his pipe made such a noise,
That he pleas'd both the girls and boys,
And they stopp'd to hear him play
"Over the hills and far away."

Tom with his pipe did play with such skill,
That those who heard him could never keep still;
Whenever they heard they began for to dance,
Even pigs on their hind legs would after him prance.

As Dolly was milking her cow one day,
Tom took out his pipe and began for to play;
So Doll and the cow danced "the Cheshire round,"
Till the pail was broke, and the milk ran on the ground.

He met old Dame Trot with a basket of eggs;
He used his pipe, and she used her legs;
She danced about till the eggs were all broke;
She began for to fret, but he laughed at the joke.

He saw a cross fellow was beating an ass,
Heavy laden with pots, pans, dishes, and glass;
He took out his pipe and played them a tune,
And the jackass's load was lightened full soon.

WHEN I was a bachelor, I lived by myself,
And all the bread and cheese I got, I put
upon the shelf;
The rats and the mice did lead me such a life,
That I went to London to get myself a wife;
The streets they were so broad, and the lanes they
were so narrow,
I couldn't get my wife home without a wheelbarrow.
The wheelbarrow broke, my wife got a fall,
Farewell, wheelbarrow, little wife, and all!

THERE was an old woman
Lived under a hill,
And if she's not gone
She lives there still.

A FARMER went trotting
Upon his grey mare;
Bumpety, bumpety, bump!
With his daughter behind him,
So rosy and fair;
Lumpety, lumpety, lump!

A raven cried "Croak";
And they all tumbled down;
Bumpety, bumpety, bump!
The mare broke her knees,
And the farmer his crown;
Lumpety, lumpety, lump.

The mischievous raven
Flew laughing away;
Bumpety, bumpety, bump!
And vowed he would serve them
The same the next day;
Bumpety, bumpety, bump!

LEG over leg,
As the dog went to Dover;
When he came to a stile,
Jump he went over.

An old woman was sweeping her house, and she found a little crooked sixpence. "What," said she, "shall I do with this little sixpence? I will go to market and buy a little pig."

As she was coming home, she came to a stile; but the pig would not go over the stile.

She went a little farther, and she met a dog. So she said to the dog—

"Dog, dog, bite pig!
Pig won't get over the stile;
And I shan't get home to-night."

But the dog would not.

She went a little farther, and she met a stick. So she said—

"Stick, stick, beat dog!
  Dog won't bite pig;
  Pig won't get over the stile,
  And I shan't get home to-night."

But the stick would not.

She went a little farther, and she met a fire. So she said—

"Fire, fire, burn stick!
   Stick won't beat dog;
   Dog won't bite pig;
   Pig won't get over the stile,
   And I shan't get home to-night."
But the fire would not.
She went a little farther, and she met some water.

So she said—

> "Water, water, quench fire!
> Fire won't burn stick;
> Stick won't beat dog;
> Dog won't bite pig;
> Pig won't get over the stile,
> And I shan't get home to-night."

But the water would not.
She went a little farther, and she met an ox.

So she said—

> "Ox, ox, drink water!
> Water won't quench fire;
> Fire won't burn stick;
> Stick won't beat dog;
> Dog won't bite pig;
> Pig won't get over the stile,
> And I shan't get home to-night."

But the ox would not.

She went a little farther, and she met a butcher.

So she said—

"Butcher, butcher, kill ox!
Ox won't drink water;
Water won't quench fire;
Fire won't burn stick;
Stick won't beat dog;
Dog won't bite pig;
Pig won't get over the stile,
And I shan't get home to-night."

But the butcher would not.

She went a little farther, and she met a rope. So she said—

"Rope, rope, hang butcher!
Butcher won't kill ox;
Ox won't drink water;
Water won't quench fire;
Fire won't burn stick;
Stick won't beat dog;
Dog won't bite pig;
Pig won't get over the stile,
And I shan't get home to-night."

But the rope would not.

She went a little farther, and she met a rat. So she said—

"Rat, rat, gnaw rope!
Rope won't hang butcher;
Butcher won't kill ox;
Ox won't drink water;
Water won't quench fire;
Fire won't burn stick;
Stick won't beat dog;
Dog won't bite pig;
Pig won't get over the stile,
And I shan't get home to-night."

But the rat would not.

She went a little farther, and she met a cat. So she said—

> "Cat, cat, kill rat!
> Rat won't gnaw rope;
> Rope won't hang butcher;
> Butcher won't kill ox;
> Ox won't drink water;
> Water won't quench fire;
> Fire won't burn stick;
> Stick won't beat dog;
> Dog won't bite pig;
> Pig won't get over the stile,
> And I shan't get home to-night."

The cat said, "If you will give me a saucer of milk, I will kill the rat."

So the old woman gave the cat the milk, and when
she had lapped up the milk—

<blockquote>

The cat began to kill the rat;

The rat began to gnaw the rope;

The rope began to hang the butcher;

The butcher began to kill the ox;

The ox began to drink the water;

The water began to quench the fire;

The fire began to burn the stick;

The stick began to beat the dog;

The dog began to bite the pig;

The pig jumped over the stile,

And so the old woman got home that night.

</blockquote>

"Come, let's to bed,"
Says Sleepy-head;
"Tarry a while," says Slow;
"Put on the pan,"
Says greedy Nan,
"Let's sup before we go."

If all the seas were one sea,
What a *great* sea that would be!
And if all the trees were one tree,
What a *great* tree that would be!
And if all the axes were one axe,
What a *great* axe that would be!
And if all the men were one man,
What a *great* man he would be!
And if the *great* man took the *great* axe,
And cut down the *great* tree,
And let it fall into the *great* sea,
What a splish splash *that* would be!

LITTLE Jack Horner,
Sat in a corner,
Eating a Christmas pie;
He put in his thumb,
And pulled out a plum,
And said, "What a good boy am I."

1.   Tʜɪѕ little pig went to market;

2.   This little pig stayed at home;

3. This little pig had roast
   beef;

4. And this little pig had none;

5. And this little pig cried,
   "Wee, wee, wee!"
   All the way home.

OLD Mother Goose, when
She wanted to wander,
Would ride through the air
On a very fine gander.

Mother Goose had a house,
'Twas built in a wood,
Where an owl at the door
For sentinel stood.

She had a son Jack,
A plain-looking lad,
He was not very good,
Nor yet very bad.

She sent him to market,
A live goose he bought,
Here, mother, says he,
It will not go for nought.

Jack's goose and her gander
Grew very fond;
They'd both eat together,
Or swim in one pond.

Jack found one morning,
As I have been told,
His goose had laid him
An egg of pure gold.

Jack rode to his mother
The news for to tell;
She called him a good boy,
And said it was well.

Jack sold his gold egg
To a rogue of a Jew,
Who cheated him out of
The half of his due.

Then Jack went a-courting
A lady so gay,
As fair as the lily,
And sweet as the May.

The Jew and the Squire
Came behind his back,
And began to belabour
The sides of poor Jack.

But Old Mother Goose
That instant came in,
And turned her son Jack
Into famed Harlequin.

She then with her wand
Touched the lady so fine,
And turn'd her at once
Into sweet Columbine.

The gold egg into the sea
Was thrown then,—
When Jack jump'd in,
And got the egg back again.

The Jew got the goose,
Which he vow'd he would kill,
Resolving at once
His pockets to fill.

Jack's mother came in,
And caught the goose soon,
And mounting its back,
Flew up to the moon.

Eena, deena, dina, duss,
Katla, weena, wina, wuss,
Spit, spot, must be done,
Twiddlum, twaddlum, twenty-one,
O U T spells out!

LADY bird, lady bird, fly away home:
Your house is on fire, your children are gone—
All but one and her name is Ann,
And she crept under the pudding-pan.

Gay go up and gay go down,
To ring the bells of London town.

Oranges and lemons,
Say the bells of St. Clement's.

Brickbats and tiles,
Say the bells of St. Giles'.

Halfpence and farthings,
Say the bells of St. Martin's.

Pancakes and fritters,
Say the bells of St. Peter's.

Two sticks and an apple,
Say the bells at Whitechapel.

Old Father Baldpate,
Say the slow bells at Aldgate.

You owe me ten shillings,
Say the bells at St. Helen's.

Pokers and tongs,
Say the bells at St. John's.

Kettles and pans,
Say the bells at St. Ann's.

When will you pay me?
Say the bells at Old Bailey.

When I grow rich,
Say the bells at Shoreditch.

Pray when will that be?
Say the bells of Stepney.

I am sure I don't know,
Says the great bell at Bow.

Here comes a candle to light you to bed,
And here comes a chopper to chop off your head.
Last, last, last, last, last man's head.

THE north wind doth blow,
And we shall have snow,
And what will Poor Robin do then?
Poor thing!

He'll sit in a barn,
And keep himself warm,
And hide his head under his wing,
Poor thing!

THERE was a crooked man, and he went a crooked mile,
He found a crooked sixpence against a crooked stile:
He bought a crooked cat, which caught a crooked mouse,
And they all lived together in a little crooked house.

HUMPTY DUMPTY sat on a wall;
Humpty Dumpty had a great fall;
All the king's horses, and all the king's men
Cannot set Humpty Dumpty up again.

UPON my word and honour,
As I was going to Stonor,
I met a pig,
Without a wig,
Upon my word and honour!

SIMPLE SIMON met a pieman,
Going to the fair;
Says Simple Simon to the pieman,
"Let me taste your ware."

Says the pieman to Simple Simon,
"Show me first your penny."
Says Simple Simon to the pieman,
"Indeed I have not any."

Simple Simon went a-fishing
For to catch a whale:
All the water he had got
Was in his mother's pail!

LITTLE Polly Flinders
Sat among the cinders,
Warming her pretty little toes.
Her mother came and caught her,
And whipped her little daughter
For spoiling her nice new clothes.

SNEEZE on a Monday, sneeze for danger;
Sneeze on a Tuesday, kiss a stranger;
Sneeze on a Wednesday, get a letter;
Sneeze on a Thursday, something better;
Sneeze on a Friday, sneeze for sorrow;
Sneeze on a Saturday, see your sweetheart
tomorrow.

WHEN the wind is in the east,
'Tis neither good for man nor beast;
When the wind is in the north,
The skilful fisher goes not forth;
When the wind is in the south,
It blows the bait in the fishes' mouth;
When the wind is in the west,
Then 'tis at the very best.

THE fair maid who, the first of May,
Goes to the fields at break of day,
And washes in dew from the hawthorn tree,
Will ever after handsome be.

There was an old woman toss'd up in a basket
Nineteen times as high as the moon;
Where she was going I couldn't but ask it,
For in her hand she carried a broom.

"Old woman, old woman, old woman," quoth I,
"O whither, O whither, O whither, so high?"
"To sweep the cobwebs off the sky!"
"Shall I go with thee?"   "Ay, by-and-by."

Four and twenty tailors went to kill a snail;
The best man among them durst not touch her tail.
She put out her horns like a little Kyloe cow;
Run, tailors, run, or she'll kill you all e'en now.

A Frog he would a wooing go,
Heigho, says Rowley,
Whether his mother would let him or no,
With a rowley, powley, gammon and spinach,
Heigho, says Anthony Rowley!

So off he sets in his opera hat,
Heigho, says Rowley,
And on the road he met with a rat,
With a rowley, powley, gammon and spinach,
Heigho, says Anthony Rowley!

"Pray, Mr. Rat, will you go with me,"
Heigho, says Rowley,
"Kind Mrs. Mousey for to see?"
With a rowley, powley, gammon and spinach,
Heigho, says Anthony Rowley!

When they came to the door of Mousey's Hall,
Heigho, says Rowley,
They gave a loud knock, and they gave a loud call.
With a rowley, powley, gammon and spinach,
Heigho, says Anthony Rowley!

"Pray, Mrs. Mouse, are you within?"
Heigho, says Rowley,
"Oh, yes, kind sirs, I'm sitting to spin."
With a rowley, powley, gammon and spinach,
Heigho, says Anthony Rowley!

"Pray, Mrs. Mouse, will you give us some beer?"
Heigho, says Rowley,
"For Froggy and I are fond of good cheer."
With a rowley, powley, gammon and spinach,
Heigho, says Anthony Rowley!

"Pray, Mr. Frog, will you give us a song?"
Heigho, says Rowley,
"But let it be something that's not very long."
With a rowley, powley, gammon and spinach,
Heigho, says Anthony Rowley!

But while they were all a merry-making,
Heigho, says Rowley,
A cat and her kittens came tumbling in.
With a rowley, powley, gammon and spinach,
Heigho, says Anthony Rowley.

The cat she seized the rat by the crown;
Heigho, says Rowley,
The kittens they pulled the little mouse down.
With a rowley, powley, gammon and spinach,
Heigho, says Anthony Rowley.

This put Mr. Frog in a terrible fright,
Heigho, says Rowley,
He took up his hat, and wished them good night.
With a rowley, powley, gammon and spinach,
Heigho, says Anthony Rowley.

But as Froggy was crossing over a brook,
Heigho, says Rowley,
A lily-white duck came and swallowed him up.
With a rowley, powley, gammon and spinach,
Heigho, says Anthony Rowley.

Taffy was a Welshman, Taffy was a thief;
Taffy came to my house and stole a piece of beef:
I went to Taffy's house, Taffy was not at home;
Taffy came to my house and stole the marrow-bone.
I went to Taffy's house, Taffy was not in;
Taffy came to my house, and stole a silver pin;
I went to Taffy's house, Taffy was in bed,
I took up the marrow-bone and flung it at his head.

There was an old woman, and what do you think?
She lived upon nothing but victuals and drink:
Victuals and drink were the chief of her diet;
Yet this little old woman could never keep quiet.

ELSIE MARLEY has grown so fine,
She won't get up to serve the swine,
But lies in bed till eight or nine,
And surely she does take her time.

LITTLE Nancy Etticoat
In a white petticoat,
And a red nose.
The longer she stands
The shorter she grows.   [*A Candle.*

MATTHEW, Mark, Luke, and John,
Bless the bed that I lie on!
Four corners to my bed,
Four angels round my head;
One to watch, one to pray,
And two to bear my soul away!

Pussy-cat, pussy-cat, where have you been?
I've been up to London to look at the queen.
Pussy-cat, pussy-cat, what did you there?
I frighten'd a little mouse under the chair.

THE man in the wilderness asked me
How many strawberries grew in the sea.
I answered him as I thought good,
As many as red herrings grew in the wood.

TELL tale, tit!
Your tongue shall be slit,
And all the dogs in the town
Shall have a little bit.

THIRTY days hath September,
April, June, and November;
February has twenty-eight alone,
All the rest have thirty-one,
Excepting leap-year, that's the time
When February's days are twenty-nine.

Poor old Robinson Crusoe!
Poor old Robinson Crusoe!
They made him a coat
Of an old nanny goat,
I wonder how they could do so!

With a ring a ting tang,
And a ring a ting tang,
Poor old Robinson Crusoe!

For want of a nail, the shoe was lost,
For want of the shoe, the horse was lost,
For want of a horse, the rider was lost,
For want of a rider, the battle was lost,
For want of the battle, the kingdom was lost,
And all for the want of a horseshoe nail.

I saw a ship a-sailing,
A-sailing on the sea;
And, oh! it was all laden
With pretty things for thee!

There were comfits in the cabin,
And apples in the hold,
The sails were all of silk,
And the masts were made of gold.

The four-and-twenty sailors
That stood between the decks,
Were four-and-twenty white mice
With chains about their necks.

The captain was a duck,
With a packet on his back;
And when the ship began to move,
The captain said, "Quack! quack!"

"ow many miles to Babylon?"—
"Threescore miles and ten."
"Can I get there by candle-light?"—
"Yes and back again!
If your heels are nimble and light,
You may get there by candle-light."

TWEEDLE-DUM and Tweedle-dee
Resolved to have a battle
For Tweedle-dum said Tweedle-dee
Had spoiled his nice new rattle.

Just then flew by a monstrous crow
As big as a tar-barrel,
Which frightened both the heroes so
They quite forgot their quarrel.

WEE Willie Winkie runs through the town,
Upstairs and downstairs in his nightgown,
Rapping at the window, crying through
the lock,
"Are the children in their beds,
for now it's eight o'clock?"

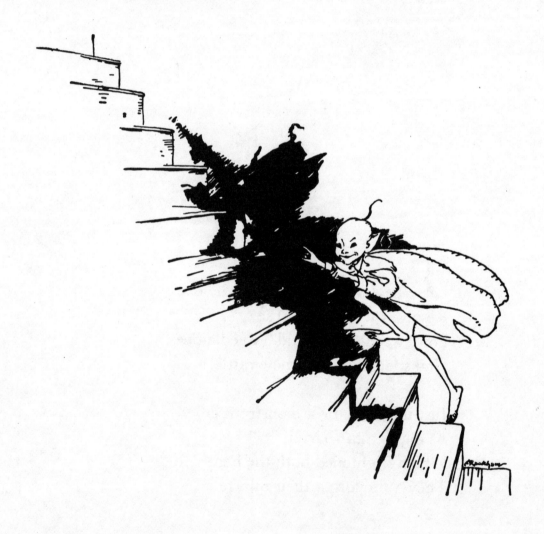

Ring-a-ring-a-roses,
A pocket full of posies,
Hush! Hush! Hush! Hush!
We all fall down.

OLD Mother Hubbard
Went to the cupboard
To get her poor dog a bone;
But when she came there
The cupboard was bare,
And so the poor dog had none.

She went to the baker's
To buy him some bread,
But when she came back
The poor dog was dead.

She went to the joiner's
To buy him a coffin,
But when she came back
The poor dog was laughing.

She took a clean dish
To get him some tripe,
But when she came back
He was smoking his pipe.

She went to the fishmonger's
To buy him some fish,
And when she came back
He was washing the dish.

She went to the ale-house
To get him some beer,
But when she came back
The dog sat in a chair.

She went to the tavern
For white wine and red,
But when she came back
The dog stood on his head.

She went to the hatter's
To buy him a hat,
But when she came back
He was feeding the cat.

She went to the barber's
To buy him a wig,
But when she came back
He was dancing a jig.

She went to the fruiterer's
To buy him some fruit,
But when she came back
He was playing the flute.

She went to the tailor's
To buy him a coat,
But when she came back
He was riding a goat.

She went to the cobbler's
To buy him some shoes,
But when she came back
He was reading the news.

She went to the sempstress
To buy him some linen,
But when she came back
The dog was spinning.

She went to the hosier's
To buy him some hose,
But when she came back
He was dress'd in his clothes.

The dame made a curtsey,
The dog made a bow;
The dame said, "Your servant,"
The dog said, "Bow, wow."

WHAT are little boys made of, made of;
What are little boys made of?
"Snaps and snails, and puppy-dog's tails;
And that's what little boys are made of, made of."

What are little girls made of, made of;
What are little girls made of?
"Sugar and spice, and all that's nice;
And that's what little girls are made of, made of."

DAFFY-Down-Dilly has come up to town
In a yellow petticoat and a green gown.

ONDON BRIDGE is broken down
Dance over my Lady Lee;
London Bridge is broken down,
With a gay lady.

How shall we build it up again?
Dance over my Lady Lee;
How shall we build it up again?
With a gay lady.

Build it up with silver and gold,
Dance over my Lady Lee;
Build it up with silver and gold,
With a gay lady.

Silver and gold will be stole away,
Dance over my Lady Lee;
Silver and gold will be stole away,
With a gay lady.

Build it up with iron and steel,
Dance over my Lady Lee;
Build it up with iron and steel,
With a gay lady.

Iron and steel will bend and bow,
Dance over my Lady Lee;
Iron and steel will bend and bow,
With a gay lady.

Build it up with wood and clay,
Dance over my Lady Lee;
Build it up with wood and clay,
With a gay lady.

Wood and clay will wash away,
Dance over my Lady Lee;
Wood and clay will wash away,
With a gay lady.

Build it up with stone so strong,
Dance over my Lady Lee;
Hurrah! 'twill last for ages long,
With a gay lady.

I F all the world was apple-pie,
And all the sea was ink,
And all the trees were bread and cheese,
What should we have to drink?

THERE was a man of Thessaly,
And he was wond'rous wise;
He jump'd into a quickset hedge,
And scratch'd out both his eyes.
But when he saw his eyes were out,
With all his might and main
He jump'd into another hedge,
And scratch'd 'em in again.

GIRLS and boys, come out to play;
The moon doth shine as bright as day;
Leave your supper, and leave your sleep,
And come with your playfellows into the street.
Come with a whoop, come with a call,
Come with a good will, or come not at all.
Up the ladder and down the wall,
A halfpenny roll will serve us all.
You find milk, and I'll find flour,
And we'll have a pudding in half an hour.

O, THE grand old Duke of York,
He had ten thousand men;
He marched them up a great high hill,
And he marched them down again!
When they were up, they were up,
And when they were down, they were down,
And when they were neither down nor up,
They were neither up nor down.

DOCTOR FAUSTUS was a good man,
He whipped his scholars now and then;
When he whipped them he made them dance,
Out of England into France,
Out of France into Spain,
And then he whipped them back again!

MARCH winds and April showers
Bring forth May flowers.

I F wishes were horses,
Beggars would ride;
If turnips were watches,
I'd wear one by my side.

S EE a pin and pick it up,
All the day you'll have good luck;
See a pin and let it lay,
Bad luck you'll have all the day!

N EEDLES and pins, needles and pins,
When a man marries his trouble begins.

Some little mice sat in a barn to spin;
Pussy came by, and popped her head in;
"Shall I come in and cut your threads off?"
"Oh no, kind sir, you will snap our heads off."

All of a row,
Bend the bow,
Shot at a pigeon,
And killed a crow.

Hot cross Buns!
Old woman runs!
One a penny, two a penny,
Hot cross Buns!

If you have no daughters,
Give them to your sons.
One a penny, two a penny,
Hot cross Buns.

As I was going to St. Ives,
I met a man with seven wives;
Each wife had seven sacks,
Each sack had seven cats,
Each cat had seven kits:
Kits, cats, sacks, and wives,
How many were going to St. Ives?

A sunshiny shower
Won't last half an hour.

Early to bed, and early to rise,
Makes a man healthy, wealthy, and wise.

The fair maid who, the first of May,
Goes to the fields at break of day

The man in the wilderness

Ring-a-ring-a-roses

As I was going to St. Ives

Tit-tat-toe,
My first go,
Three jolly butcher-boys,
All in a row;
Stick one up,
Stick one down,
Stick one in the old man's crown.

One, two, three, four,
Mary at the cottage door;
Five, six, seven, eight,
Eating cherries off a plate.
O U T spells out!

Cock-a-doodle-doo!
My dame has lost her shoe;
My master's lost his fiddling-stick,
And don't know what to do.

Cock-a-doodle-do!
What is my dame to do?
Till master finds his fiddling-stick,
She'll dance without her shoe.

Cock-a-doodle-doo!
My dame has lost her shoe,
And master's found his fiddling-stick;
Sing doodle-doodle-doo!

Cock-a-doodle-doo!
My dame will dance with you,
While master fiddles his fiddling-stick,
For dame and doodle-doo.

DEEDLE, deedle, dumpling, my son John
Went to bed with his trousers on;
One shoe off, the other shoe on,
Deedle, deedle, dumpling, my son John.

As Tommy Snooks and Bessy Brooks
Were walking out one Sunday,
Says Tommy Snooks to Bessy Brooks,
"Tomorrow will be Monday."

HERE am I, little jumping Joan.
When nobody's with me,
I'm always alone.

I HAD a little pony,
His name was Dapple-grey
I lent him to a lady,
To ride a mile away.
She whipped him, she slashed him,
She rode him through the mire;
I would not lend my pony now
For all the lady's hire.

THERE was an old woman called Nothing-at-all,
Who rejoiced in a dwelling exceedingly small;
A man stretched his mouth to its utmost extent,
And down at one gulp house and old woman went.

CURLY locks! curly locks! wilt thou be mine?
Thou shalt not wash dishes, nor yet feed the swine,
But sit on a cushion and sew a fine seam,
And feed upon strawberries, sugar and cream!

FIDDLE-DE-DEE, fiddle-de-dee,
The fly shall marry the humble-bee.
They went to the church, and married was she:
The fly has married the humble-bee.

ROBIN and Richard were two pretty men;
They lay in bed till the clock struck ten;
Then up starts Robin and looks at the sky,
Oh! brother Richard, the sun's very high:

You go first with bottle and bag,
And I'll come after on little Jack Nag;
You go first and open the gate
And I'll come after, and break your pate.

A RED sky at night is a shepherd's delight,
A red sky in the morning is a shepherd's
warning.

A CARRION crow sat on an oak,
Fol de riddle, lol de riddle, hi ding do,
Watching a tailor make a cloak.
Sing heigh, sing ho, the carrion crow,
Fol de riddle, lol de riddle, hi ding do.

Wife bring me my old bent bow,
Fol de riddle, lol de riddle, hi ding do,
That I may shoot yon carrion crow.
Sing heigh, sing ho, the
carrion crow,
Fol de riddle, lol de riddle,
hi ding do.

The tailor shot, but he missed his mark,
Fol de riddle, lol de riddle, hi ding do,
And shot the old sow right through the heart.
Sing heigh, sing ho, the carrion crow,
Fol de riddle, lol de riddle, hi ding do.

THE rule of the road is a paradox quite,
Though custom has prov'd it so long;
If you go to the left, you go right,
If you go to the right, you go wrong.

LITTLE boy blue, come, blow up your horn,
The sheep's in the meadow, the cow's in the corn.

THREE wise men of Gotham
Went to sea in a bowl:
And if the bowl had been stronger,
My song would have been longer.

Two legs sat upon three legs,
With one leg in his lap;
In comes four legs,
Runs away with one leg,
Up jumps two legs,
Catches up three legs,
Throws it after four legs,
And makes him bring back one leg.

[*One leg is a leg of mutton; two legs, a man; three legs, a stool; four legs, a dog.*]

OLD King Cole
Was a merry old soul,
And a merry old soul was he;
He called for his pipe,
And he called for his bowl,
And he called for his fiddlers three.

Now every fiddler, he had a fiddle,
And a very fine fiddle had he;
Twee tweedle dee, tweedle dee, went
the fiddlers.
Oh, there's none so rare,
As can compare
With King Cole and his fiddlers three!

Old King Cole
Was a merry old soul,
And a merry old soul was he;
He called for his pipe,
And he called for his bowl,
And he called for his harpers three!

Now every harper he had a harp,
And a very fine harp had he;
Twang, twang, twang, went the harpers,
Twee tweedle dee, tweedle dee went
the fiddlers.
Oh, there's none so rare,
As can compare
With King Cole and his harpers three!

Old King Cole
Was a merry old soul,
And a merry old soul was he;
He called for his pipe,
And he called for his bowl,
And he called for his trumpeters three.

Now every trumpeter he had a trumpet,
And a very fine trumpet had he;
Tantara, tantara, went the trumpeters,
Twang, twang, twang, went the harpers,
Twee tweedle dee, tweedle dee went
the fiddlers.
Oh, there's none so rare,
As can compare
With King Cole and his trumpeters three!

Old King Cole
Was a merry old soul,
And a merry old soul was he;
He called for his pipe,
And he called for his bowl,
And he called for his pipers three.

Now every piper he had a pipe,
And a very fine pipe had he;
Whew, whew, whew, went the pipers,
Tantara, tantara, went the trumpeters,
Twang, twang, twang, went the harpers,
Twee tweedle dee, tweedle dee, went
the fiddlers.
Oh, there's none so rare,
As can compare
With King Cole and his pipers three!

Old King Cole
Was a merry old soul,
And a merry old soul was he;
He called for his pipe,
And he called for his bowl,
And he called for his fifers three.

Now every fifer he had a fife,
And a very fine fife had he,
Tootle, tootle, toot, went the fifers,
Whew, whew, whew, went the pipers,
Tantara, tantara, went the trumpeters,
Twang, twang, twang, went the harpers,
Twee tweedle dee, tweedle dee, went
the fiddlers.
Oh, there's none so rare,
As can compare
With King Cole and his fifers three!

Old King Cole
Was a merry old soul,
And a merry old soul was he;
He called for his pipe,
And he called for his bowl,
And he called for his drummers three.

Now every drummer he had a drum,
And a very fine drum had he;
Rub-a-dub-dub went the drummers,
Tootle, tootle, toot, went the fifers,
Whew, whew, whew, went the pipers,
Tantara, tantara, went the trumpeters,
Twang twang, twang, went the harpers,
Twee tweedle dee, tweedle dee, went
the fiddlers,
Oh, there's none so rare,
As can compare
With King Cole and his drummers three!

WHO killed Cock Robin?
I, said the Sparrow,
With my bow and arrow
I killed Cock Robin.

Who saw him die?
I, said the Fly,
With my little eye
I saw him die.

Who caught his blood?
I, said the Fish,
With my little dish
I caught his blood.

Who'll make his shroud?
I, said the Beetle,
With my thread and needle
I'll make his shroud.

Who'll dig his grave?
I, said the Owl,
With my spade and trowel
I'll dig his grave.

Who'll carry him to the grave?
I, said the Kite,
If it's not in the night
I'll carry him to the grave.

Who'll carry the link?
I, said the Linnet,
I'll fetch it in a minute,
I'll carry the link.

Who'll sing a psalm?
I, said the Thrush,
As he sat on a bush,
I'll sing a psalm.

Who'll be chief mourner?
I, said the Dove,
I'll mourn for my love,
I'll be chief mourner.

Who'll be the parson?
I, said the Rook,
With my little book,
I'll be the parson.

Who'll be the clerk?
I, said the Lark,
If it's not in the dark,
I'll be the clerk.

Who'll toll the bell?
I, said the Bull,
Because I can pull,
I'll toll the bell.

All the birds in the air
Fell a-sighing and a-sobbing,
When they heard the bell toll
For poor Cock Robin.

A FOX started out in a hungry plight,
And begged of the moon to give him light,
For he'd a long way to go that night
Before he could reach the downs, O!
Downs, O! Downs, O!
For he'd a long way to go that night
Before he could reach the downs, O!

The Fox when he came to the farmer's gate,
What should he see but the farmer's black duck!
"I love you," says he, "for your master's sake,
And I long to be picking your bones, O!
Bones, O! Bones, O!
I love you," says he, "for your master's sake,
And I long to be picking your bones, O!"

Then he seized the black duck by the neck,
And swung her all across his back,
The black duck cried out, "Quack! Quack! Quack!"
With her legs hanging dangling down, O!
Down, O! Down, O!
The black duck cried out, "Quack! Quack! Quack!"
With her legs hanging dangling down, O!

Old Mother Slipper-slopper jumped out of bed,
And out of the window she popped her old head,
Crying, "John, John, John, the black duck is gone,
And the Fox has run off to his den, O!
Den, O! Den, O!
John, John, John, the black duck is gone,
And the Fox has run off to his den, O!"

Then John, he went up to the top of the hill,
And blew his horn both loud and shrill.
Says the Fox, "That is very pretty music, still
I'd rather be safe in my den, O!
Den, O! Den, O!"
Says the Fox, "That is very pretty music, still
I'd rather be safe in my den, O!"

At last Mr. Fox got home to his den,
To his dear little foxes, eight, nine, ten,
Says he, "We're in luck, here's a fine fat duck,
With her legs all dangling down, O!
Down, O! Down, O!"
Says he, "We're in luck, here's a fine fat duck,
With her legs all dangling down, O!"

Then the Fox sat down with his cubs and his wife;
They did very well without fork and knife,
Nor ate a better duck in all their life,
And the little ones picked the bones, O!
Bones, O! Bones, O!
They never ate a better duck in all their life,
And the little ones picked the bones, O!

INDEX OF FIRST LINES